# Ghost Po

Chosen by
John Foster

## Contents

| | | |
|---|---|---|
| The Haunted House | *John Foster* | 2 |
| What's That? | *John Foster* | 4 |
| The Night Visitor | *Ann Bonner* | 6 |
| The Shadow Man | *John Foster* | 8 |
| The House at Night | *James Kirkup* | 10 |
| Ghostly Lessons | *Judith Nicholls* | 14 |
| Who's Afraid? | *John Foster* | 15 |
| The Boastful Ghost | *Richard Edwards* | 16 |

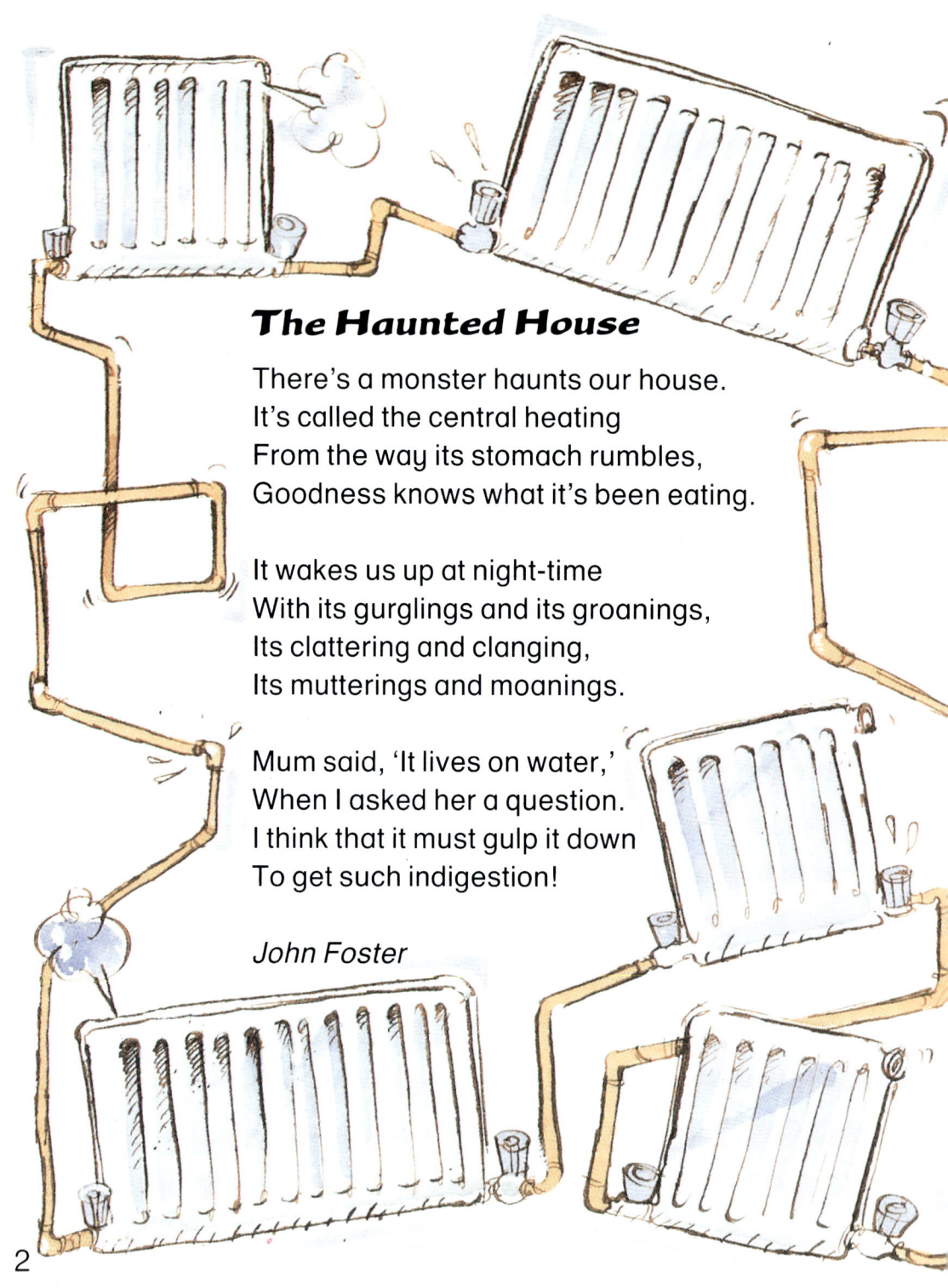

### The Haunted House

There's a monster haunts our house.
It's called the central heating
From the way its stomach rumbles,
Goodness knows what it's been eating.

It wakes us up at night-time
With its gurglings and its groanings,
Its clattering and clanging,
Its mutterings and moanings.

Mum said, 'It lives on water,'
When I asked her a question.
I think that it must gulp it down
To get such indigestion!

*John Foster*

## What's That?

What's that rustling at the window?
Only the curtain flapping in the breeze.

What's that groaning in the garden?
Only the branches swaying in the trees.

What's that rattling at the front door?
Only the wind in the letter-box flap.

What's that drumming in the bathroom?
Only the dripping of the leaking tap.

What's that hissing in the front room?
Only the gas as it burns in the fire.

What's that murmur in the kitchen?
Only the whirring of the tumble drier.

What's that shadow lurking
   in the corner beside the door?
It's only your clothes where you left them
   lying on the bedroom floor.

*John Foster*

# The Night Visitor

Some
THING
went
bump
in the
night.

THUMP
in the
night.
Gave
me a
fright.

A shadow
moved
on the
wall.
Long-
legged
and
terribly
tall.

A ghoulie?
Or
ghostie
in white?
A trick
of the
light?

No.
Nothing
went
bump
but that
BEASTLY

lump
of a
cat.
Asleep!
On my
bed.

She
made me
jump
last night.

*Ann Bonner*

# The Shadow Man

At night-time
As I climb the stair
I tell myself
There's nobody there.

But what if there is?
What if he's there —
The Shadow Man
At the top of the stair?

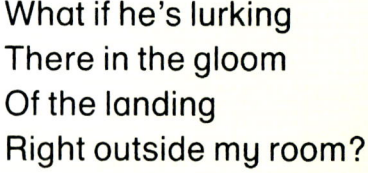

What if he's lurking
There in the gloom
Of the landing
Right outside my room?

The Shadow Man
Who's so hard to see
What if he's up there
Waiting for me?

At night-time
As I climb the stair
I tell myself
There's nobody there.

*John Foster*

# The House at Night

When it grows dark
We go to our beds,
And nothing exists
But the dreams in our heads.

Yet while we're asleep
The house soon awakes:
It rustles and rattles
And shudders and shakes!

The drainpipes gurgle,
The windowpanes sigh,
The floors toss and turn
And the chimneypots cry.

The house sounds as if
It's taking a break,
With time off from *us*
And the racket we make.

So it stretches its arms
And relaxes a while.
And on its old face
There's a sly little smile.

It flings up its tiles
And lets down its hair,
Then does a wild tap-dance
Up and down stair.

And sometimes if you
Wake up in the night
You can catch it at play,
And it gives you a fright

To hear it go bong,
Clatter, giggle and beep,
So you shut your eyes tight,
Try to go back to sleep.

But when the alarm goes
At seven o'clock,
The house's mad antics
Suddenly stop!

And you wonder a while –
Is the house all it seems?
All those weird goings-on!
Or were they just dreams?

*James Kirkup*

## Ghostly Lessons

Mum, I want some chocolate,
just one little treat –
peppermint or strawberry cream . . .

GHOSTS DON'T EAT!

Mum, I've got a toothache,
a pain beneath my heel;
my throat's too sore to work tonight. . .

GHOSTS DON'T FEEL!

Mum, I really hate the dark –
I hate the way they stared!
I'm scared of graveyards, woods and folk . . .

GHOSTS AREN'T SCARED!

*Judith Nicholls*

# Who's Afraid?

Do I have to go haunting tonight?
The children might give me a fright.
It's dark in that house.
I might meet a mouse.
Do I have to go haunting tonight?

I don't like the way they scream out,
When they see me drifting about.
I'd much rather stay here,
Where there's nothing to fear.
Do I have to go haunting tonight?

*John Foster*

### The Boastful Ghost

The boastful ghost flapped through a wall,
His white face full of glee,
'I'm much the bravest ghost there is,
A real ghoul,' said he,
'All living creatures great and small
Are terrified of me.'

Just then a bustling, bright-eyed mouse
Came hopping down the stair,
The ghost looked round, shrieked: 'Help!' and flew
To tremble on a chair,
And, passing by, the tiny mouse
Was heard to squeak: 'Oh yeah?'

*Richard Edwards*

**Read along with me**

# Samson's Taste of Honey

Colin and Sheila Smithson

**Marshall Pickering**

Samson lived when his land was ruled by a strange people — the Philistines.

The Philistines were great warriors who landed on the coast from the sea. They had better weapons than the Israelites and soon defeated them. Then they took away their swords. They even took away their blacksmiths to stop them making new weapons.

At the wedding Samson taunted the Philistine family. He asked them an impossible riddle. But his new wife told her family the answer.

He had been tricked!

Samson felt foolish!

In a rage he killed thirty Philistines.

Samson's fights with the Philistines grew worse and worse until the Philistine generals declared war on the Israelites. There was about to be a battle.

So the Philistines made peace and Samson was made ruler of his people.

The Philistines would wait their chance to bring down Samson.

He ruled for twenty years. He eventually fell in love again. This time with Delilah.

Delilah was as sweet as honey.

But Delilah had been persuaded by the enemy to discover the secret of Samson's great strength. In return they would give her a huge amount of money.

Delilah's strength was her sweetness. She quizzed Samson until he gave in.

"If my hair is cut – I would be no stronger than any other man."

Delilah set a trap. While he slept, Samson's hair was cut.

And sure enough, Samson lost his strength.

He was captured.

They made him blind and set him to work in the corn mill in the great prison.

But with time Samson's hair began to grow and as it grew so did his strength.

The Philistines celebrated their victory over the Israelites. They held a festival to their god – the "god of the sea".

Thousands of people crowded into the temple to make fun of their great enemy – Samson.